PEOPLE IN THE PAST

Ancient Greek Women

Haydn Middleton

Heinemann
LIBRARY

www.heinemann.co.uk/library
Visit our website to find out more information about **Heinemann Library** books.

To order:
☎ Phone 44 (0) 1865 888066
▤ Send a fax to 44 (0) 1865 314091
▢ Visit the Heinemann Bookshop at www.heinemann.co.uk/library to browse our catalogue and order online.

First published in Great Britain by Heinemann Library, Halley Court, Jordan Hill, Oxford OX2 8EJ, a division of Reed Educational and Professional Publishing Ltd. Heinemann is a registered trademark of Reed Educational & Professional Publishing Ltd.

OXFORD MELBOURNE AUCKLAND JOHANNESBURG BLANTYRE
GABORONE IBADAN PORTSMOUTH NH (USA) CHICAGO

Designed by Tinstar Design (www.tinstar.co.uk)
Illustration by Art Construction.
Originated by Ambassador Litho Ltd.
Printed by Wing King Tong in Hong Kong.

ISBN 0 431 14542 3
06 05 04 03 02
10 9 8 7 6 5 4 3 2 1

British Library Cataloguing in Publication Data
Middleton, Haydn
   Ancient Greek women. - (People in the past)
   1. Women - Greece - To 1500 - History - Juvenile literature
   2. Greece - Civilization - to 146 B.C. - Juvenile literature
   I. Title
   305.4'0938

Acknowledgements
The Publishers would like to thank the following for permission to reproduce photographs:
AKG London pp6, 7, 12, 17, 18, 19, 24, 25, 26, 28, 39, Ancient Art and Architecture Collection pp10, 11, 15, 20, 22, 29, 32, 34, 36, 40, 42, Bildarchiv Preussischer Kulturbesitz p43, Performing Arts Library p38, Werner Forman Archive pp8, 30.

Cover photograph reproduced with permission of the Metropolitan Museum of Art.

Every effort has been made to contact copyright holders of any material reproduced in this book. Any omissions will be rectified in subsequent printings if notice is given to the Publisher.

The Publishers would like to thank Dr Michael Vickers of the Ashmolean Museum, Oxford, for his assistance in the preparation of this book.

Words appearing in the text in bold, **like this**, are explained in the Glossary.

Contents

The ancient-Greek world

'So Plato gave thanks to nature, first that he was born a human being rather than a dumb animal; second that he was born a man rather than a woman.'

So wrote Lactantius, about the great **philosopher** Plato. Plato was by no means the only ancient Greek who believed that men were 'superior' to women. Aristotle, who was famed for his scientific ideas, wrote: 'A woman is … an imperfect male. She is female because her body is not properly made.'

Plenty of other books and laws show a similar male attitude towards women. Unfortunately, hardly any writings by women about men have survived. In fact we have hardly any women's writings from those times about *anything*. As a result, ancient Greece seems to have been very much a man's world.

From Minoans to Macedonians

When people talk about ancient Greece, they do not just mean the modern country of Greece as we know it today. The ancient-Greek world was made up of the hot, rocky mainland of Greece, plus hundreds of islands in the Aegean, Ionian and Adriatic Seas, with further overseas **colonies** in places ranging from northern Africa to what we now call Turkey and Italy. The earliest Greek-speakers did not think they all belonged to a single country. For a long while they did not even think they all belonged to the same **civilization**.

For centuries the mightiest people in the Greek world were the Minoans, based on the island of Crete. Power then passed to the warlike Mycenaeans, based in the mainland region known as the **Peloponnese**. This was followed around the year 1100 BC by three centuries of confusion and upheaval; since the art of writing was also lost, we know very little about it. In the Classical Age that followed (from about 500 to 300 BC), prosperity was restored by the rise to power of a number of long-lasting city-states including Athens, Sparta and Thebes. Most of the information in this book is about the life of women in city-states like these during this period of Greek history.

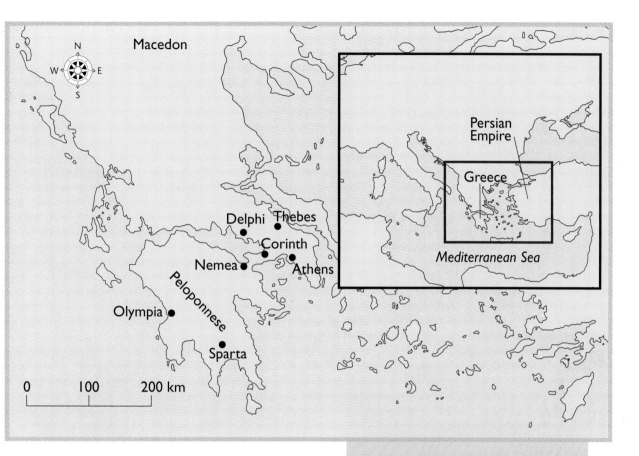

The Greek word for city-state was **polis**. Each *polis* controlled the villages and farmland around it. Each also had its own laws and customs, and often they fought bitter wars against each other. However, all Greeks were united by their common language and by a belief that their ways were superior to those of any foreign **barbarians**. The quality of many aspects of their civilization makes it hard to disagree. Today – more than two thousand years since the Greek world was finally united under King Alexander the Great of Macedon, before becoming a part of the Roman Empire in 146 BC – ancient-Greek words, ideas, art-forms and attitudes still have a deep effect on us all.

Ancient Greece was not a single unified country but a collection of many separate states that varied greatly in size and strength. The ancient Greeks used the word *Hellas* to mean all the places where there was a Greek way of life.

The second sex?

Many ancient Greeks believed that the world was made up of 'opposites'. There were Greeks and there were non-Greeks (whom they called **barbarians**). There were free people and there were slaves. There was right and there was left. There were men and there were women. Greeks believed that within each of these pairs, the first was not only different from the second, it was also better. It is hard for us to understand this today. It seems offensive that men should be thought *better* than women. Yet this apparently strange idea had a deep influence on life in ancient Greece.

Well-kept secrets

In reporting a speech by Pericles, the historian Thucydides recorded this rather uninspiring statement about female virtues: 'If I am also to speak about feminine virtue … I can say all I have to say in one short word of advice. Your great glory is not to be inferior to the way nature made you; and the greatest glory is hers who is least talked about by men, whether in praise or in blame.' Athenian men were also expected to keep the names of their female family members secret from any men who were not related to them.

In Greek art, women were often shown to be small and inactive when compared to men. Unlike men too, they were almost always shown clothed!

Some Greek men feared that there was a 'wild streak' in all women. Images like this one suggested their 'beastly' side, unless they were kept under strict control – by men of course!

Gender differences

As you will discover in this book, Greek writers and artists had strong views on the differences between the sexes, and on the different roles they had to play. Whereas a man was expected to enjoy an active public life, a woman's place was thought to be in the home. Sometimes it may seem to you that women had a really hard time. Even in city-states like Sparta, where women had more freedom, they seemed able to do and say far less than men.

Surviving sources tell us very little about everyday life in ancient Greece and many of these sources tell us only how men *wanted* women to behave, not how they actually led their lives. We must use the evidence carefully if we are to glimpse what life was really like for women – and bear in mind that not *all* Greek men feared or disliked women. As Xenophon wrote: 'The god of nature has given different kinds of beauty to us. It is his wish that the magnificence of the male should be admired by the female, and that the tender and curious touch of the female should be admired by the male'!

Greek girls

The two girls in the statuette below are playing knucklebones – a popular game for Greek children. Girls also played with painted clay spinning tops, dolls and rattles. We know this because such items are sometimes found by **archaeologists** in the graves of children who died young. Maybe they were placed there for playing with in the next world.

Just like today, the number of toys a girl had depended on how wealthy her family was. So did the amount of time that she was allowed to play with them. The daughters of poor farmers had to work from a very early age – scaring birds away from crops, or helping with the harvest. Like today too, children kept pets: but hares and quails rather than gerbils or budgies!

These girls are playing knucklebones. There were no mass-produced toys in ancient Greece so children often had to make the best of what came to hand.

Becoming adult early

Childhood did not last long – for boys or girls. Boys went to school but girls did not. Girls seem to have been brought up almost entirely inside their homes. There they learned the skills they would one day need to run a household of their own – like weaving, spinning, cooking and looking after children.

From around the age of thirteen, girls were not considered to be children themselves any more. During a special **ritual** they dedicated all their toys to the goddess Artemis, before putting them aside forever. They married young, then continued the cycle by producing more babies.

In some states, if a child was born weak or sickly its father could refuse to bring it up. Then it would be exposed – left in a public place to die or be adopted by someone else. It is possible that more girl babies than boy babies were treated in this way. Fathers may have welcomed male children more, since they could go out into the world and bring fame or wealth to the family. Most girls did not work for pay, so they had to be supported. From about 500 BC, their families also had to provide them with a **dowry** before they could be married.

Girls on the left

Today, 'gynaecology' is the scientific study of women's bodies and diseases. It comes from the Greek word *gyne*, meaning woman. Ancient-Greek scientists had some bizarre ideas about what went on inside women's bodies. Girl babies were said to grow on the left of the womb, boys on the right. Some Greek doctors also thought that the womb could roam around inside a woman – from her stomach, to her chest, to her head!

Becoming a wife

The author Xenophon wrote out a conversation between Ischomachos, a wealthy country squire, and Socrates the **philosopher**. 'Pray tell me,' asks Socrates, 'did you instruct your wife how to manage your house, or was it her father and mother that gave her sufficient instructions to order a house before she came to you?' 'My wife,' answers Ischomachus, 'was but fifteen years old when I married her; and till then she had been so negligently brought up, that she hardly knew anything of worldly affairs.' Isomachus nonetheless expected his young wife to start taking charge of the household immediately.

This is a picture of a wedding procession, by the Athenian painter Exekias from about 540 BC. Only rich newly-weds could afford horse-drawn chariots like this one. The rest had to be tugged along by less expensive mules or oxen.

Love *and* marriage?

In ancient Greece, fifteen was not especially young for a bride. Grooms tended to be older – in their late twenties at least – and were often already close to the bride's family: a cousin or a father's best friend. Most marriages were arranged by parents, and a girl might be **betrothed** while still a child.

For the Greeks, the 'purpose' of being female was to be married and the purpose of marriage was to have children to keep the family going. That might not sound very romantic. Indeed, few people seem to have married for love. One reason why a man married a girl was because she was expected to bring him a **dowry**. (The richer the girl's family, the greater her dowry was likely to be. It could be as much as ten per cent of her father's wealth or property.) Love did then sometimes grow up inside a marriage.

Inscriptions on tombs suggest that there could be affection between **spouses**, and in pictures of wedding ceremonies the gods of love are often shown. These ceremonies did not take place in temples. The groom fetched the bride from her home and took her in a chariot or cart back to his family's house. There the groom's parents met them, led them to the **hearth** – the symbol of family life – and showered them with fruit and nuts. The couple knelt by the fire to say prayers and then the next day there was a feast with present giving.

Early ends to marriage

Since a bride was usually much younger than her new husband, she was often by far the youngest person in her new household. It must have been hard to adjust – especially as she had to spend so much time indoors (see page 12). For marriages that did not work, divorce was a way out. If a man divorced his wife, he had to pay back her dowry, and then she normally returned to her own family home. If the father of an **heiress** died however, Athenian law said she *had* to divorce her husband then marry her nearest available relative, to make sure that all her father's property would not be shared out among distant family members.

This beautifully-decorated *loutrophoros* pot was used to fill the **ritual** bath of a bride before her wedding. A pot like this might also be placed, as a marker, on the grave of any woman who never got married.

A woman's place

'There is one prime source of scandal
for a woman, when she won't stay indoors.
I longed to go out, but no! I stayed at home
and indoors I didn't practice saucy speech,
like some women. My mind, sound by nature,
was my teacher. I needed no more.
I offered my husband a silent tongue
and gentle looks. I knew when to have my way and
when to let him have his.'

This speech tells us a lot about women's roles in Greek families. It is made by Andromache in *The Women of Troy*, a play written by Euripedes. The playwright, a man, was putting words into the mouth of a woman. Yet women really were expected to stay out of sight and mind their tongues while they managed their husbands' households. Andromache, however, suggests that she knew how to manage her husband too: 'letting' him have his way, and 'knowing' when to have her own.

Here, a Greek woman washes and beautifies herself. In her domestic setting, a Greek wife and mother was the Queen Bee – but she was given little chance to 'buzz around' out of doors.

Maybe some women had quite a lot of power at home. We cannot say for sure, since there is so little surviving evidence. In Xenophon's play *Oeconomicus* Socrates asks Kritoboulos 'Is there anyone to whom you commit more affairs of importance than to your wife.' 'No,' he replies. Then Socrates asks, 'Is there anyone to whom you talk less?' 'Few or none,' he admits. This suggests that Kritoboulos was quite happy to leave his wife to get on with organizing his home.

Buried alive in the hive

The verse-writer Semonides of Amorgos likened women to different types of animal. Only a woman like a bee is any good for a man: 'She causes his property to grow and increase, and she grows old with a husband whom she loves and who loves her, the mother of a handsome and **reputable** family. She stands out among all women, and a godlike beauty plays around her. She takes no pleasure in sitting among women in places where they tell stories about love.' Bees, of course, are famously busy – and wives and mothers, whether rich or poor, had their work cut out in running a household. There would have been little time for them to do jobs outside the home or get involved in politics. This suited many men perfectly. For they believed that the temptations of the outside world would be too strong for most women to resist.

Mothers and children

'Plainly,' wrote Xenophon in *Memorabilia*, 'we look to wives who will produce the best children for us, and marry them to raise a family … She cares for the baby night and day laboriously for a long period, and with no expectation of reward.' Greek fathers do not seem to have been very hands-on! A Greek woman might have six or seven pregnancies, but maybe as many as one in three babies died in their first year. Poor women, unable to afford the expense of looking after them, sometimes gave up their babies for adoption.

Mistress of the household

The Greek word for a home was *oikos*. As well as meaning the brick, stone or unbaked clay that the house was built from (most Greek homes were very simply made), it also meant the family who lived inside it. Today, we might use the word 'household' to mean something similar. Sometimes three generations would live under a single roof: grandparents, a married son and his wife, then their children. In larger homes there might even be more relatives – either unmarried, widowed or divorced. Although the head of the *oikos* was always a man, the task of making it run smoothly fell to the women – whether they were members of the family or, in richer homes, maidservants or slaves.

Andron and *gunaikon*

On the following pages you can find out what jobs women had to do, or supervise. They did their work in several different kinds of home, but in many the women's own quarters were **segregated** from the men's more public areas – especially the *andron*, where male guests were entertained.

The women's area of the house was called the *gunaikon*. In bigger Athenian houses, women's rooms were not near the street entrance, which might be guarded by a slave porter. In country farmhouses there were courtyards where the women and children lived by day, surrounded by single-storey rooms. In one corner there might be a storage tower. If a stranger or male visitor came, the women would retreat into its upper rooms.

Women below

'I have a small two-storey house, with the women's quarters upstairs, the men's downstairs, each having equal space. When our son was born, his mother nursed him; but in order that she might avoid the risk of climbing downstairs each time she had to clean the baby, I used to live upstairs and the women below. And so it became quite customary for my wife to go downstairs often and sleep with the child, so that she could give him the breast and keep him from crying.' (Lysias)

This seated woman must have been quite wealthy, since she is being waited on by a female servant. Rich wives were expected to train and supervise their domestic staff. 'We're always dancing attendance on our husbands,' says a character in Aristophanes' play *Lysistrata*, 'or getting the maid moving, or putting the baby to bed, bathing it, feeding it.'

Chief cook and bottle washer

The women's quarters in a Greek house included the cooking area. Men, maidservants or slaves went shopping for food but women did most of the cooking. In towns women had to make bread – a vital part of the diet – from barley. 'Take care that the corn which is brought in,' Ischomachus advised his wife in Xenophon's *Oeconomicus*, 'is not laid up in such a manner that it grows musty and unfit for use.' Barley was usually soaked and toasted before it was turned into porridge or cakes. A bride might bring a barley-roasting pan to her wedding.

Women from reasonably wealthy families prepared only one big meal a day, the *deipnon*, which was eaten in the late afternoon. The first course might consist of poultry or fish, with maybe some cheese, accompanied by sauces and by vegetables like lentils, celery, radishes and beans. A second course could include figs, olives, grapes, nuts and other fruit. Cattle were in short supply, and meat of any kind was usually eaten only at the feast after a **sacrifice**.

How to eat and drink

Greek people followed various **rituals** for eating and drinking. The **philosopher** Plutarch said that when he was growing up, girls and boys were trained to take bread with the left hand and *opson* (almost everything else) with the right. There was also no shortage of advice on how to drink the strong, gritty wine (beer was drunk only by **barbarians**).

Women drank water, wine, or more usually a mixture of the two. Sometimes they drank in the company of men but they were seldom invited to parties called *symposia*, which could get a little wild. Women were supposed to drink enough diluted wine to make them feel relaxed and chatty, but not so much that it made them 'stupid'.

Finding the right balance

Women had to take care over what types of food they put together and exactly how they cooked them. Each dish had a particular 'power' over the body, it could be: 'moistening', 'drying', 'heating', 'sweet', 'fatty' or 'strong'. Unfortunately, not everyone agreed on which foods had which powers!

Honey was keenly sought out by women who could afford it. The god Zeus was said to have been brought up on honey and goat's milk.

Women from all backgrounds were likely to include fish on their menus. From anchovies and sprats to tuna, sea bass, red mullet and eels, fish in huge numbers were harvested from the rich seas around Greece, so they were relatively cheap.

This statuette shows a Greek woman preparing a meal. There were few labour-saving devices in the kitchens of the ancient world, although slaves and servants did some of the more demanding work.

Family Fates

In ancient-Greek mythology, there were three sister goddesses, known as the Fates. These three Fates were in charge of human destiny. Clotho spun out the thread of each person's life, Lachesis measured how long that thread should be, and Atropos chose when to cut it and so bring death.

Wool and women

For **mortal** Greek women, spinning and weaving in the home were very important occupations. Although the rich might *buy* clothes of linen, hemp, flax or silk, many ordinary Greek families kept a few sheep to provide wool for making their own garments. The women of the household would dye it and spin it into **yarn** before weaving it into cloth to make whatever was needed. This could be a wall-hanging or floor-covering or an item of bedding as well as clothes.

Not *all* cloth was made in the home by women. Some was made in small 'factories' where men worked too, but wool and women usually went together. In Athens, when a baby girl was born a **fillet** of cloth was attached to the house's main door to announce the good news. Athenian women also took part in the *Panathenaea* festival each year by weaving a new dress for Athena, the city's protecting goddess. There was even a story that all Athenians were actually *descended* from a piece of wool!

Decorative images like this one on a vase often showed women spinning or weaving.

Penelope's deception

Women wove cloth by standing or sitting at upright wooden **looms**. It could take a long time. In Greek myth, Odysseus the King of Ithaca was away from his wife Penelope for twenty years. Many suitors gathered at her palace, saying he must be dead and hoping to marry her instead. Penelope said she would choose a new husband when she had finished weaving a **shroud** for Odysseus's father. Each day she worked at her loom, but each night in secret she unpicked her day's work. By doing this, she played for time – and in the end Odysseus returned to her.

This decorated item was called an *epinetron*. Women used it to tease out tangled wool before they started to spin it.

Work outside the home

The wives of wealthy Greek men rarely ventured beyond their homes. Their husbands thought it far too risky. According to the playwright Aristophanes, if a woman even stood at her door on to the street, she was thought to be tempting men inside! Aristotle wrote that in some classical cities, officials called *gunaikonomoi* supervised wealthy women and made sure they stayed indoors. Women like these would not even visit the market to buy fresh food, or corn to make bread. Such jobs would be done instead by their menfolk, or else by maidservants and slaves.

This young woman is entertaining a group of men by playing a wind instrument. Other ancient-Greek paintings show female musicians playing hand-held harps and dancers performing expressive steps.

Citizens and slaves

In 5th-century Athens there were between 80,000 and 100,000 slaves. That was one slave for every free member of the population. Most of them were foreign – **Persians** or Asians captured during warfare. Some were just the children of slave-parents.

Slaves in Sparta, Thessaly or Sicily often led hard lives, but in Athens it could be difficult to tell who was a slave and who was free. At the marketplace, slaves rubbed shoulders with poor women who had no one to run their errands for them. Sometimes, to make money, these poor women sold foods from their family gardens at the market too. They might also work outside the home as cooks, cleaners, nannies, **wet-nurses**, grape-pickers or barmaids.

Younger poor women might perform in other people's homes as paid dancers or musicians. Some girls played an instrument called an *aulos*, which was something like a modern oboe. At the lower end of its range, the Greeks said it sounded like the buzzing of wasps, while on the high notes it was like the honking of geese. Men were still happy to pay to hear it played!

Struck off the register

Slaves and women did not qualify as **citizens**, who were allowed to vote. This meant that they had no say in how their city-state was run. Citizens and their families were not supposed to do 'common' jobs. However, in times of crisis and hardship, some free-born citizens did soil their hands with work. At the end of the **Peloponnesian** War with Sparta, it was discovered that the mother of an Athenian, Euxitheous, had been working as a 'petty trader' and wet-nurse. As a result, Euxitheous was struck off the register of citizens. 'You will find many Athenian citizens acting as wet-nurses today,' Euxitheous protested. '... Of course if we were rich we should not now be selling ribbons; we should not need to. But what has this to do with my family's position as free-born Athenians?'

Letting their hair down

Life was not all work and no play for Greek women. Yet if their husbands preferred them not to go out, what did they do for entertainment? Men were able to go to the theatre, to watch plays written by men and performed by men. Women were not supposed to be in these audiences. Yet Plato wrote that some 'refined' women did watch public plays, and that they preferred **tragedies** to comedies. Some women spectators were, however, terrified by one of Aeschylus's plays.

Euripides wrote a play, *The Bacchai*, about the maddened drunken female followers of the god Dionysos, shown here. 'I have stung them with frenzy,' claims Dionysos in the play, 'hounded them from home up to the mountains where they wander, crazed of mind.' Some Greek men feared that *all* women could be tempted like this.

Mystery festival

Most women probably enjoyed themselves by visiting, or being visited by, female friends or relatives. In the privacy of their own homes they could 'let their hair down'. How *much* they let their hair down is another matter. Male Greek writers thought women lacked any self-control and said they easily fell in love or got drunk. Can we believe this? Aristotle said that in Sparta, where women had more freedom than in some other city-states, 'women live without restraint, enjoying every **licence** and indulging in every luxury.'

Holy dances

The ancient Greeks believed that they had invented dancing. Women did not dance in a casual way, but at religious festivals they performed in public and enjoyed watching others perform. Sometimes women danced in procession to the temples of the gods. The celebrations might also include singing, drinking wine and eating barley-cakes. Women let their hair down especially in honour of the god Dionysus – performing an outdoor 'mountain-dance' that followed a winding torchlit path up through the trees.

Men were also suspicious about what went on at all-female festivals like the *Thesmophoria* (see pages 32–33). In a play by Aristophanes, a man dresses up as a woman and tries to take part. The women will not let him, unless he can say what happens at the festival:

Women: Tell me, what do we do first as part of the holy **rites**?
Man: Er, let me see, what is it first? – we drink.
Women: Well, what do we do after that?
Man: We drink.
Women: Someone must have been letting on to you …

Aristophanes was only guessing what happened at the festival. Even today we have no real idea what went on! We do have a clearer picture of how men let their hair down. At their all-male dinner parties, girl musicians would sometimes perform for the guests, playing wind or stringed instruments. At least girls like these were given the chance to get out and about.

What they wore

Paintings and figures from ancient times show us clearly what Greek women wore. Male artists often portrayed boys and men naked, but almost always showed women with their clothes on. This may have meant they believed women's bodies were shameful or 'abnormal'. Or it may have meant they found women even more attractive when they were 'veiled' from view.

The classical style

Ancient Greece was a hot place. Many Greek women just wore a *chiton*, a long, sometimes-patterned, loose-fitting linen **shift** without sleeves. It was held in place by brooches at the shoulder and by a belt, at or above, the waist. This produced the folds often shown in Greek sculpture. In colder weather, well-off women might then wear a square of woollen cloth on top as a cloak. This was called a *himation*. On their feet they wore simple leather sandals with nailed soles, made by a local cobbler. Wealthier women probably had their clothes made for them, and had a number of different outfits to choose from. More usually, women wove clothes for the whole family at home.

We can get clues about what women wore from sculptures like these from the Erechtheion, a temple built high above Athens.

24

Clothes like these were fairly loose and shapeless – unlike those of **barbarians** who were often shown in tight-fitting outfits that showed off their bodies. Variety came from the materials used for *chitons* – hemp, linen, silk, wool – and from the different decorative styles, whether striped, spotted or bordered. Colours also varied; yellow was thought to be 'feminine'.

Then, like today, some people used tricks to improve their appearances. This comes from *Fair Measures* written by the comic poet Alexis: 'One is rather short. A cork sole is stitched into her shoes. One is too tall. She wears thin slippers … One has no hips. She sews on a bustle under her dress.' Xenophon advised against paying attention to any sort of clothing: 'Those who study nothing but their dress may be esteemed by those who understand nothing else. But the outside appearance is deceitful.'

This vase painting shows women harvesting fruit. It would lead us to believe that the robes they are wearing are the everyday dress of women in ancient Greece.

Unsuitably dressed

According to one Greek source, if a woman was seen on the streets of Athens in 'unsuitable' clothing, she could be made to pay a fine of 1000 *drachmas*. We cannot be sure what 'suitable' clothing was, but it probably kept the body well covered. The **philospher** Socrates once argued with his wife Xanthippe because she refused to wear his big cloak when going out to watch a festival procession. Yet when women took part in weddings or great festivals in public, they dressed up in fine clothes, gold and jewels.

Beauty tips

'The face that launched a thousand ships, and burned the topless towers of Ilium.' That is a description of Helen, one of the most famous women in Greek myth. She was so beautiful that a quarrel over who should be her husband sparked off the ten-year-long war between Greece and Troy (or Ilium). So how did **mortal** Greek women beautify themselves? As usual, men had their own ideas.

Keep it simple

Xenophon's Ischomachus liked the clean and simple look: 'Men always prefer that body which is most pure, or the least deformed by art.' He recommended housework to make a woman look 'more healthful … and add to the bloom' of her beauty.

It is hard to know whether the artist was intending to show how lovely this Greek woman looked, or how vain she was about her appearance. Some male writers seemed to prefer women with a more 'natural' look.

Then, 'the clean appearance of the mistress among the servants …
will encourage them to follow her example.' Aristophanes wrote
that some women wore so many ornaments that he couldn't
possibly list them all: 'Some face powder, some scent … a veil,
some **rouge**, two necklaces, some eye paint … a hair-net …
earrings, a pendant, more earrings … pins, necklet, armlet, bangles
… anklets, seals, chains, rings … *more* earrings – it's past man's
power to tell you all the things.'

Men had clear ideas on
women's skin-tones too. Women
were believed to take in more
moisture from their food, so
their flesh was 'wetter and wool-
like'. Also, as you can see in
paintings, Greek men are usually
shown with darker skins, while
women (and 'womanish'
barbarians!) are shown pale
and white. Maybe men wanted
to keep them indoors to stop
them getting suntans.

Women wore perfume from
little bottles called *aryballoi*.
Rich women used scents
imported from abroad. Local
mixtures were made from olive
oil and herbs. Unless they were
slaves, women wore their hair
long – in ringlets before they
were married, then piled up
with ribbons and metal
decorations afterwards. Just like
today, styles and lengths went in
and out of fashion.

Keeping up appearances

In *Fair Measures*, the comic poet
Alexis described how some women
tried to disguise flaws in how they
looked, while others made the best of
their assets:

'One has blonde eyebrows. They
paint them with lampblack.

One is too dark-complexioned; she is
smeared with white-lead.

One is too pale; she applies rouge.

One is beautiful – in part. That part is
revealed bare.

One has attractive teeth. She must
always be laughing so that those
present can see what a nice mouth
she has.

If she doesn't want to laugh, she has
to spend the whole day indoors, and
like the stuff on the butcher's counter,
when they are selling goat's head, she
has to keep a slim stick of **myrtle**
vertically between her lips, till as time
passes, she's grinning whether she
wants to or not.'

Goddesses

'All things,' said the **philosopher** Thales, 'are full of gods.' The people of ancient Greece worshipped many different **deities** – some private or local, some that 'ruled' over the entire Greek world. The Greeks believed that six major gods and six major goddesses 'lived' on Mount Olympus, at 2917 metres, the highest mountain in Greece.

Both men and women prayed to the goddesses – Hera, Athene, Aphrodite, Demeter, Artemis and Hestia – but all six had special powers for women. Hera, Zeus' wife and queen of the gods, was the guardian of faithful wives. Athene watched over crafts like spinning and weaving, among other duties. Aphrodite was the goddess of love. Demeter, the goddess of fertility, made sure that the earth brought forth an abundance of crops. Artemis protected unmarried girls and watched over women in childbirth. Hestia watched over the most important place in most women's lives – home and **hearth**. Many stories or myths survive that feature these goddesses. From them we can gather what 'ideal' Greek women were supposed to be like.

This statue, from about 130 BC, shows the Venus de Milo. Milo was the Roman name for Melos, the Greek island where the statue was found. Venus was the Roman name for Aphrodite, the Greek goddess of love.

The judgement of Paris

In a famous Greek myth, Paris, the handsome son of the King of Troy, is given a golden apple. He is told by the god Mercury to give it to the most beautiful of three goddesses – Athene, Hera or Aphrodite. Each goddess, desperate to win, offers Paris a gift if he will pick her. Athene says she will make him invincible in battle. Hera promises to make him lord over all Asia or all men. Aphrodite says she will give him the loveliest of all **mortal** women, Helen, to be his wife. Paris picks Aphrodite and gives her the apple. Soon afterwards he meets Helen, who is already married to the Greek King Menelaus, seizes her and takes her back to Troy. The tug-of-love that followed resulted in the ten-year-long Trojan War. The Greeks sometimes used myths like this to explain real-life events.

Guardian of Greece's greatest city

Although the women of Athens had no say in running their city, its **patron** was a female deity – Athene. As the goddess of wisdom and warfare, she was supposed to ensure that the men of Athens governed wisely and fought well. The Greek sculptor Phidias made a famous statue of Athene, 12 metres high and covered in gold, ivory and coloured stones, which stood in the Parthenon temple.

Athene herself had no real mother (see caption below). To be a true Athenian **citizen** (that is, someone who could vote in elections and help to run the city) men had to have both an Athenian father *and* an Athenian mother.

This vase shows the goddess Athene who, according to legend, sprang fully-formed and already dressed in armour from the head of her father Zeus.

Troublemakers

Odysseus – tied to the ship's mast by his own men – becomes the first man to hear the song of the evil female Sirens and live to tell the tale.

This picture shows a scene from Greek mythology. The man is Odysseus, King of Ithaca. His thrilling story is told in the *Odyssey* by the poet Homer who probably wrote between 800 and 700 BC. Odysseus has several encounters with female troublemakers. In this scene he has asked to be tied to the mast, for he knows that beautiful creatures called Sirens lure sailors to their doom with irresistible songs. Odysseus wants to hear the Sirens, but not be able to go to them. The men in his crew have their ears stuffed with beeswax so that they cannot hear.

Bogey-women

Myths explore people's deepest fears and longings. In the Greek myths, men often described what they thought women *might* be like if they were not kept under strict control. The lovely, **seductive** but evil Sirens are an example.

Another nightmare figure is Medusa, a 'Gorgon' with snakes for hair and a mouth filled with tusks. Anyone who looked her in the face was turned to stone. Then there were the Harpies, monstrous birds with women's faces and long hooked claws. They swooped down to ruin the food people were eating, and sometimes carried off the people themselves. More threatening still were the Amazons, who could out-do men as warriors: 'they were considered men on account of their courage rather than women on account of their physical nature.' Some said they even removed one breast so they could fire their arrows more easily. There were no men in their nation. If any Amazon gave birth to a son, he was either killed or sent to live with his father in one of the neighbouring lands.

Stories about creatures like these were meant to be entertaining. They also served as warnings about the dangers lurking in all women – and helped to 'explain' why women had to be kept in their place by men.

Giving in to temptation

Pandora – believed by the Greeks to be the first **mortal** woman – was created by several **deities**. Zeus then gave her a jar or box which he ordered her never to open. Once on Earth, she married a man called Epimetheus, but she could not resist the temptation of looking inside the box to see what was there. As soon as she opened it, Disease, War, Famine and all the other evils poured out, to trouble the world forever after. Only blind Hope remained, to bring comfort to trouble-struck mankind. One message of this Greek myth is: men need women, but women are bound to make life difficult.

Women out in public

Greek women were supposed to be weaker than men – more emotional, less **rational**, and therefore more prone to wild behaviour. This generally led men to keep them closely supervised. However, on *some* occasions the 'weaknesses' of women came in handy. At funerals and religious festivals they could express their emotions in public – and leave the men to maintain their usual strong 'manliness'.

These women are tying ribbons to a tombstone as part of a funeral ceremony.

Keeping in with the gods

Many different local and national festivals were held in honour of Greek **deities**. The Greeks believed that the gods watched what went on, and as a result treated the people taking part more favourably. This was not exactly rational behaviour, so women played a major role in many of the **rituals**. The great *Thesmophoria* festival, held for three days in Athens each autumn, was celebrated *only* by women. At the *Arrephoria*, unmarried girls celebrated strange **rites** to bring about fertility. Pausanias, who wrote a *Guide to Greece* in c.150 BC, described them in this way:

'Two girls live near the temple of Polias; the Athenians call them *Arrephoroi*. They are boarded for a time with the goddess. When the festival comes round they perform the following ritual by night. They set on their heads objects given them to carry by the priestess of Athene; the nature of these objects is not known to either giver or bearers. Now there is within the city not far away an enclosure dedicated to the goddess called Aphrodite in the Gardens, and there is a natural underground passage leading down through it. The girls make their descent by this. They leave down below the objects they are carrying, and bring back something else which is carefully wrapped up. The girls are then dismissed.' Weird, and probably very scary – definitely women's work in the eyes of many Greek men!

Funeral practices

Greek art clearly shows that women took the chief role as **mourners** during funeral processions to the cemetery. Laws were passed in Athens to limit women's **lamentations** for the dead; for fear that they might cause a public disturbance. Euripides described women mourners in this way: 'Mothers have lost their children, maidens have cut their hair in mourning for their brothers … Hands are laid to the head; fingernails tear the delicate skin of the cheek which is wet from the flowing of blood.' By contrast, the menfolk stayed largely silent while the body was laid out to be visited by people paying their last respects, then taken to the cemetery for burial.

Women at the Olympics

A great athletic festival took place every four years to honour the god Zeus. Since it was held at Olympia in the **Peloponnese** it became known as the Olympic Games. According to tradition, the Games were founded by Heracles, and the first Olympic champion was Coroebus of Elis – a local cook who won the sprint race in 776 BC. Coroebus was a man. So were all the other competitors, whether runners, jumpers, chariot-racers, horse-racers, boxers, wrestlers, discus throwers or javelin throwers. So were the spectators.

Apart from a few priestesses, women were most definitely not welcome. Even women-owners of chariots or horses were forbidden to enter the sacred arena to watch them compete.

A Spartan girl athlete would have been given more freedom than elsewhere in Greece to participate and compete in athletic events. It was believed that if girls trained hard, they would make themselves 'strong for childbirth' when they were older.

Crazy Callipateira

Since their presence was seen as **sacrilegious**, any woman who was caught in the crowd could be punished by execution. However, this did not put off one woman, whose story was told by several Greek writers.

Callipateira of Rhodes belonged to a family of successful athletes in the 5th century BC. Her father and three brothers all won Olympic crowns. In due course, her own son Eukles showed great promise as a boxer. Callipateira longed to see him take part in the Games, so she dressed herself as a male trainer and slipped into the stadium. When Eukles became the Olympic champion, Callipateira could not contain her joy. She leapt out of the crowd to embrace her beloved son – and so revealed herself to be a woman!

The officials debated what to do with her. In the end they let her off, out of respect for her distinguished family. However, from that point on all trainers had to be naked, to prevent any more deception. This was not quite so startling as it might sound – for all the athletes themselves competed in the nude.

Female athletes

At the main Olympic Games only men were allowed to compete for prizes and glory. There were races for young women at other times. At Olympia there was a very old temple to the goddess Hera, wife of Zeus. Its officials trained girl athletes who then ran short races in honour of the goddess. Women did finally make it into the main Olympics – but they had to wait until the 20th century before men let them in. The ancient Olympics were abolished in AD 393, then revived on an international basis in 1896. At those first 'modern' Olympics, held in Athens, women were still not permitted to compete, but from 1900 that all changed – and the athletes wore clothes too!

Women with names

Greek men were not supposed to discuss their womenfolk in public. Even saying the women's names could be **taboo** (see page 6). Likewise, male Greek writers have left us with very few descriptions of the lives of real women, but we do know about three: Xanthippe, Aspasia and Sappho.

Many stories were told about Xanthippe, the nagging wife of the **philosopher** Socrates. He often seemed weary of her. On the morning of his execution, wrote Plato, 'we went in and found Xanthippe sitting by him with their child in her arms. When Xanthippe saw us she burst out with the sort of sentiments women will produce: "Socrates, this is the last time you and your friends will talk together." Socrates looked towards Crito and said, "Crito, someone had better take her home."' Maybe he was just being kind.

This Athenian vase from the 5th century BC shows Sappho, the celebrated female poet from the island of Lesbos. Her skills were valued so highly that parents living elsewhere in Greece sent their daughters to be taught by her.

Aspasia and Sappho

Aspasia lived in Athens in the 5th century BC. A clever, strong-minded woman, she entertained many great Athenian men in her home – and, unusually at that time, took part in their 'man-talk'. One of them, the political leader Pericles, fell in love with her, divorced his wife and set up a new home with her. People believed she helped him to write many of his great speeches. To some men, this did not seem like a suitable role for a woman and they criticized her bitterly. Yet Pericles stood by her until his death. 'Every day,' wrote Plutarch 'on leaving for his public business and on returning he would kiss her.'

Sappho, a poet, was a rare Greek woman whose *own* writings have survived. We know little about her life – she was born in about 600 BC on the island of Lesbos, and was married with a daughter. She may have thrown herself off a cliff for the love of a young boatman. Her poems were praised in her lifetime and have inspired many other great writers, both ancient and modern.

Passionate poetry

'Whenever I look at you even quickly

it is no longer possible to speak,

but my tongue fixes, and at once

a delicate fire flickers under my skin.

'I no longer see with my eyes, my ears hum,

sweat trickles down me, trembling seizes me all over,

I am paler than grass, and I seem to be

little short of dying.'

That is one of Sappho's most famous love poems. Another fragment, found on **papyrus** and also about deep feelings, begins like this:

'Some say that the most beautiful thing on this dark earth

is a squadron of cavalry, others say

a troop of infantry, others a fleet of ships:

but I say that it is the one you love.'

Tragic women

'The lot of women is troublesome to men and since the good are confused with the bad, we are all hated. Thus we are born unlucky.' So says Kreousa in *Ion*, a drama by Euripedes. Kreousa is a fictional character but, as in many Greek plays by men, she gives us a glimpse of how women saw their lives.

In *Tereus*, a **tragedy** by Sophocles, Procne makes this sad speech: 'In my opinion young girls have the sweetest existence known to **mortals** in their fathers' homes – innocent, safe and happy always. But when we grow a little older, we are thrust out and sold away into marriage. Some go to strangers' homes, others to foreigners', some to joyless houses, some to hostile. And as soon as we have been yoked to our husbands, we are forced to say all is well.'

The Irish actress Fiona Shaw plays Medea in a terrifying modern version of Euripides' play about the mythical woman who murdered her children.

The eternal outsider

In his play about the mythic witch Medea, Euripides showed just how wild a woman could be. For Medea killed her own children to punish her husband Jason for abandoning her. The playwright also put words into Medea's mouth that expressed how hard women's lives were (see below). Medea, from distant Colchis, was a **barbarian** herself – an outsider among the Greeks. Many Greek plays showed *all* women being treated like outsiders, like creatures that brought only turmoil into the 'civilized' world of men.

Women's tribulations

In this speech from the play about her by Euripides, Medea speaks out for the hardships many Greek women suffered:

'Of all creatures that feel and think,

we women are the unhappiest species …

When the man tires of the company of his wife,

he goes outside and relieves the burden of his heart

and turns to a friend or companion of his own age.

But we are forced to keep our eyes on one alone.

They say that we women have a safe life at home,

while men must go to war. Nonsense!

I would rather fight in the battle line three times

than go through childbirth once.'

The figure of Medea continues to haunt the imaginations of creative artists in modern times. In 1998 the German author Christa Wolf wrote a wonderful novel about her.

Did women get a fair deal?

The women of Athens had far fewer rights than most women today. They were seldom supposed to leave the home, let alone do jobs or have a say in the way that the **polis** was governed. No women had the vote or were allowed to speak at the public **assembly**. Nor were they allowed inside the law courts. For the whole of their lives they were subject to a male 'guardian'. So when they got married, they passed from dependence on their father (or closest male relative) to their husband. If they got divorced or were widowed, they then had to go back under the control of the men of their blood family. One of the few advantages in being female was that you did not have to fight in wars.

This woman is shown in a respectful pose towards a man, but many Greek men seem to have felt threatened by women and by their inner 'wildness'.

The Spartan exception

Elsewhere in ancient Greece, women held a similar **status**. A woman's guardian had to feed, clothe and protect her, but in return she was like a piece of his property.

It was, however, a different story in the *polis* of Sparta. There, since men aged up to 30 lived together in special military **barracks**, many women had to manage their households alone. They could own land and property, take part openly in outdoor sports and even express their views on current affairs! The thinker Aristotle was unimpressed by these arrangements: 'At Sparta women live without restraint, enjoying every **licence** and indulging in every luxury. One inevitable result is that great importance is attached to being rich, particularly in communities where the men are dominated by the women.'

To us, it seems that most ancient-Greek women were second-class citizens. Many women today would find it hard to live under such conditions. We can try to guess what Greek women thought about their lot in life – but since so little hard evidence of their views survives, we cannot know for sure.

It is also worth remembering that in many other parts of the world, until very recent times, women were equally 'unfree'. According to the historian Oswyn Murray, 'the position of Athenian women was in most important respects the same as that of the 200 million women who live today under Islam.'

The value of discipline

Greek men believed in discipline. They themselves needed it as well as women. Without it, they feared, there would be chaos in the world. Yet while men had taught themselves to 'live decently', women continued to behave wildly. That was why they needed even stricter, continuous discipline from men. Kreon, a male character in one of Sophocles' plays puts it this way:

'There is no greater wrong than disobedience.

This ruins cities. This tears down our homes,

this breaks the battle-front in **panic-rout**.

If men live decently it is because

discipline saves their lives for them …

I won't be called weaker than womankind.'

How do we know? – Delphi

The landscape of Greece is still littered with ruins from ancient times. Along with surviving Greek art and the work of Greek writers, this archaeological evidence often helps historians to form a clearer picture of the past. We know from Greek writings that Delphi (see map on page 5) was supposed to be at the exact centre of the world. In a steam-filled cave there, the Greeks set up the ancient world's most famous **oracle**. The most important person in this most sacred and important of places was … a woman.

Pithy sayings of the Pythia

You might be surprised that a woman, not a man, presided at Delphi. In this book you have found out how small a part most women played in public life. Greek men believed that since women were so 'emotional', they could be very dangerous. So they tried to keep them hidden away and gave them few rights. Yet they also thought that by being so emotional, women were in closer touch with the supernatural. Therefore they were better able than **rational** men to make contact with the gods, and to listen to what they wanted **mortals** to do.

So, according to writers, on the seventh day of each month a high priestess called the Pythia would sit on a sacred tripod in a trance amid 'holy' vapours. She would listen to the enquiries of visitors from all over the ancient world, then give answers 'inspired' by the god Apollo.

This is an aerial view of the site of Delphi today. Two pieces of general advice from the god Apollo were carved on the front of the Temple: one was 'Know yourself' and the other was 'Nothing too much'.

These answers were not always straightforward, and had to be 'interpreted' by male priests (see box). Yet, in male-dominated Greece, it was a woman who held one of the 'top jobs'!

We do not rely on writings alone for our information on Delphi. Alongside the oracle was built a Temple to Apollo, an amphitheatre, a stadium to hold the Pythian Games and the treasuries of Greek cities that helped to pay for their upkeep. In 331 AD, Aristotle and his nephew made a list of all the champions at the Pythian Games. These records were **inscribed** on four stone tablets that were found by **archaeologists** in modern times.

Today we can visit the ruins of this sacred site in its beautiful location, following in the footsteps of countless **petitioners** who came with their urgent enquiries for the Pythia. In some ways the ruins themselves are now like oracles, opening up to us the secrets not of the future, but of the past.

This painting from around 440 BC shows the priestess Pythia sitting on the sacred tripod in a trance. Perhaps the man pictured here is waiting for answers!

These are two responses given by the Pythia to enquiries at Delphi:

● King Croesus of Lydia wanted to know whether to go to war or keep the peace. The Pythia said: GO TO WAR AND DESTROY A GREAT EMPIRE. Croesus went to war, and his own empire was destroyed.

● The Romans, Lucius Junius Brutus and two companions, asked what the future held for them. The Pythia said: YOUNG MEN, HE AMONG YOU WHO FIRST SHALL KISS HIS MOTHER WILL HOLD THE HIGHEST POWER IN ROME. Brutus bent down to kiss the ground (*Mother* Earth). In 509 BC, he became First Consul of Rome, the city's chief **magistrate**.

Timeline

All dates are BC

c.3000	Greece controlled till c.1450 by Minoan kings based on the island of Crete
c.1600–1100	Greek-speaking Mycenaeans rule separate kingdoms in mainland Greece
c.1100–800	Period of wars and migration
c.800–700	Homer's the *Iliad* and the *Odyssey* probably composed; Greece made up of city-states, ruled by separate kings or noble families
c.750–550	Greeks set up colonies in lands around Mediterranean
c.600	Birth of female poet Sappho
c.580	First major temple of Athene built in Athens
c.500	Some city-states become democracies – Athens the most powerful
c.490–479	Main period of **Persian** invasions of Greece
438	Statue of Athene dedicated at Parthenon
431–404	**Peloponnesian** War between Greek city-states ends with Sparta eclipsing Athens as most powerful state in mainland Greece
c.431	Euripedes' play *Medea* performed
378–371	Sparta eclipsed by a new power – Thebes
336–323	Greece ruled by Alexander the Great of Macedon after his invasion and conquest
146	Greece becomes part of the Roman Empire

Sources

Ancient Greece – Utopia and Reality
Pierre Lévêque
(Thames Hudson, 1994)

Classical Greece
Ed. Roger Osborne
(Oxford University Press, 2000)

Eat, Drink and be Merry
Audry Briers
(Ashmolean Museum, 1990)

Europe – A History
Norman Davies
(Oxford University Press, 1996)

Greece and the Hellenistic World
Ed. John Boardman, Jasper Griffith and Oswyn Murray
(Oxford University Press, 1988)

The Greeks
Paul Cartledge
(Oxford University Press, 1993)

Political and Social Life in the Great Age of Athens
Ed. John Ferguson and Kitty Chisholm
(Ward Lock, 1978)

These Were the Greeks
H.D. Amos and A.G.P. Lang
(Hulton, 1979)

Women in Athenian Law and Life
Roger Just
(Routledge, 1989)

Glossary

archaeologists people who learn about the past by studying old buildings and objects

assembly gathering of Athenian citizens who governed the city

barbarian word used by Greeks to describe anyone who was not Greek

barracks buildings where soldiers live

betrothed engaged, promised in marriage to someone

citizen people with political rights, never a woman

civilization way of life common to a particular group of people

colonies settlements in one place made by people from another place

deities gods and goddesses

dowry property or money brought by a bride to her new husband

fillet narrow band for binding the hair

hearth floor of a fireplace and the area around it

heiress woman who inherits or will inherit property or wealth

inscriptions words written on stone, a monument or a coin

lamentations grief-stricken wailing

licence freedom or permission to do something

looms machines for weaving yarn or thread into fabric

magistrate officer in charge of enforcing the law

mortal living creature or human, that can die. The opposite of the immortal gods who lived forever.

mourners people who grieve after a loved-one has died

myrtle plant with dark leaves, white scented flowers and black berries

oracle place where people could ask their gods for advice or prophecies

panic-rout kind of chaos caused by fear

papyrus material used for writing on, made from reeds

patron protecting figure

Peloponnese region of southern Greece, including Sparta
(see map on page 5)

Persian person who lived in the ancient Middle-Eastern kingdom of Persia, now
known as Iran

petitioners people who ask or 'petition' for help or advice

philosopher seeker after wisdom, often a teacher of great knowledge

polis Greek word for city-state

rational sensible, sane

reputable respectable

rites special celebrations, often at a religious festival

ritual special, often holy, way of doing something

rouge substance used for colouring lips and cheeks

sacrifice ritual slaughter and cooking of an animal in honour of a god

sacrilegious offensive to something sacred, against holy law

seductive appealing in a tempting way

segregated kept apart

shift woman's loose-fitting dress

shroud cloth used for wrapping up a corpse

spouses husbands and wives

status position in society

taboo forbidden thing

tragedies serious plays about serious subjects

wet-nurses woman employed to feed a baby with her own milk

yarn any kind of thread that has been spun

Index

Titles in the *Ancient Greek* series include:

Hardback   0 431 14550 4

Hardback   0 431 14541 5

Hardback   0 431 14543 1

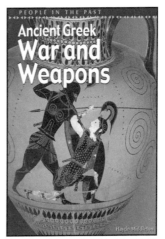

Hardback   0 431 14540 7

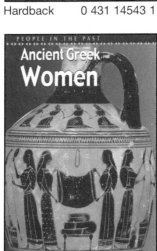

Hardback   0 431 14542 3

Find out about the other titles in this series on our website www.heinemann.co.uk/library